The Right to be Ridiculed

Andrew Conway

O&U
Onwards & Upwards

Onwards and Upwards Publishers

3 Radfords Turf, Cranbrook, Exeter,
EX5 7DX, United Kingdom.
www.onwardsandupwards.org

First edition, published in the United Kingdom by Onwards and Upwards Publishers (2019).

ISBN: 978-1-78815-746-9
Typeface: Sabon LT
Graphic design: LM Graphic Design

Printed in the United Kingdom.

About the Author

Andrew Conway is a disciple of the Lord Jesus who has occasionally had the privilege of being ridiculed for the Master. He is also privileged to be Sarah-Jayne's husband; Annie and Peter's father; and the minister of Hilltown and Clonduff Presbyterian Churches in County Down. He is passionate about honouring Christ in the whole of life, including his hobbies of reading and woodwork.

To contact the author, please write to:

Andrew Conway
c/o Onwards and Upwards Publishers Ltd.
3 Radfords Turf
Exeter
EX5 7DX

More information about the author can be found
on the book's web page:

www.onwardsandupwards.org/the-right-to-be-ridiculed

Endorsements

This is a timely treatment of the eighth beatitude for today's church. Andrew Conway has served us all well by reminding us that Jesus did not evade the issue of alerting his disciples, of all ages, to the likelihood of ridicule and worse because they follow him.

He goes on to anchor that reality in the present, embracing opposition in the local situation and persecution in the world church.

With careful argument, shot through with spiritual insights from Puritan thought, he sets forth the incomparable privilege of knowing Jesus which makes any ridicule or persecution 'worth it all'.

The doctrine he sets out is followed by detailed application to everyday discipleship. Flowing from our loving response to the Lord, our response to everyone else, fellow believers and those who oppose us, is painstakingly worked out in terms of personal reaction to others, character building, sharing in fellowship, engaging in worship and supremely, in becoming Christlike.

Stephen's reaction, as he was martyred, is used to encourage us that the same Holy Spirit can enable us to reflect Christ when we are ridiculed, or worse.

This book stirred my mind, enflamed my heart and challenged my attitudes profoundly. I unhesitatingly commend it to you with the prayer that your love for Christ will be similarly enhanced.

S. John Dixon
Former Moderator of the Presbyterian Church in Ireland

I found this to be a prophetic book, in the sense that I've got to get much better at enduring hostility as I proclaim Jesus as Lord. Andrew Conway, by thinking this issue through so deeply, has done a great service to today's church.

Buckle up, hostility is coming!

Rico Tice
Co-founder of Christianity Explored Ministries

The Right to be Ridiculed is a great reminder that, whether you are imprisoned in a North Korean camp for reading your Bible or ostracised at the water cooler for talking about God at your workplace, Jesus is absolutely worth it. This book will help you embrace, and maybe even look forward to, ridicule on your journey to become more Christ-like.

Eddie Lyle
President of Open Doors UK and Ireland

The Right to be Ridiculed

Contents

Foreword by Michael A. Barry

When I was elected as Moderator Designate of the Presbyterian Church in Ireland, one of my first tasks was to find someone to take charge of the congregation for the year of my absence. That is normally offered to an Assistant Minister of the Church who is ready to receive a call. Having taken advice from others who knew those in such a position, the name of Andrew Conway was one which kept cropping up. Having met with Andrew personally, I was willing to suggest he meet with our Kirk Session. They were unanimous in supporting my view that he would be a suitable replacement. So he 'held the fort' for thirteen months in my absence.

To say he did a good job would be to undervalue Andrew's ministry in Newry. Towards the end of his time, in the light of my impending retirement more than one person was heard to say, "Is there no way we can keep him?" Indeed, Andrew had carried on a most faithful and acceptable ministry in the congregation and community. Andrew was loved by all – not only because of his personality but also his teaching ministry. He was faithful to the Word, fearless in his proclamation, practical in his application, and all done with a spirit of love for his Lord and the people.

This book which you hold deals with a subject which is becoming more prevalent today. As society becomes more secular, it becomes more godless and more antagonistic to the things of God. How are believers to react, especially to the ridicule which may be poured on them? With anger? With retaliation? With fear? Perhaps the simplest thing is to hide away and not let anyone know about our faith.

Yet as Andrew clearly shows in this book, none of these are helpful to us or, more importantly, honouring to God. So how should we react when we are the subject of ridicule because we follow Jesus? The Bible has answers to that question and here you will not only learn what the Bible has to say but also how to apply that teaching to your own soul. This is a very practical book as befits one who adheres to classic Reformed teaching and method, and those who read it and apply its teaching will find their souls blessed and be better equipped to face the challenges of living for Christ in a hostile world today.

Michael A. Barry
Former Moderator of the Presbyterian Church in Ireland

Introduction

In the aftermath of the horrific terrorist attack on the offices of *Charlie Hebdo* magazine in January 2015, some of us found ourselves contemplating 'the right to ridicule'. Footage showed one of the attackers shouting, 'We have avenged the prophet!' – an outlandish claim which no doubt caused great offence to many, but which also cast some light on the motive of the terrorists.

Charlie Hebdo is a satirical magazine which many people find amusing, but which often gives offence to others. Religious people, in particular, are often hurt by the way in which the magazine portrays either their particular faith or religion in general. Needless to say, the vast majority have reacted in a much more sensible and decent fashion than the terrorists mentioned above. While no right-thinking person would ever come any way close to imaging that there could be any kind of justification for the terrorist attacks, there nevertheless remains a real question as to whether or not *Charlie Hebdo*'s satirical publications regarding religion are morally appropriate. Some would argue that mocking the sincerely held beliefs of others (religious or otherwise) is not a compassionate course of action, and therefore it's not a fitting one to take. This viewpoint certainly has merit.

It's in response to this line of argument that the so called 'right to ridicule' makes an appearance. Some would argue that where beliefs are manifestly ridiculous, people ought to have the right to bring this to light by ridiculing them. Indeed, it might even be possible to argue that this is a kind and caring thing to do. Some believe that you can treat people compassionately by ridiculing beliefs they hold dear, provided your goal is to rescue them from such thinking. Parents and teachers at times have employed this approach to encourage the young people under their care to reconsider their views.

I find this whole argument fascinating. I've no doubt that at times in the past I've ridiculed false beliefs in the course of my teaching ministry (I trust, with a loving and compassionate motivation). Christian leaders and teachers of standing and influence far beyond mine have certainly employed ridicule. Moreover, there is at least some weight to the suggestion that the practice has a biblical basis. Elijah surely ridiculed the beliefs of the prophets of Baal in 1 Kings 18:27. Might it even be fair to say that the Lord himself – the man of a pure, compassionate heart like no other – ridiculed the false beliefs of the Pharisees, in Matthew 23:24-28, for example?

Yet this apparent biblical basis might be open to challenge. If the Lord Jesus did indeed ridicule false belief, he obviously did so rightly, but that doesn't necessarily mean that he gives others the right to do so too. The Lord can rightly do things which his followers have no right to do and ridiculing false beliefs may be one such thing. Of course, this doesn't make him guilty of hypocrisy – it's no more hypocritical than a mother telling her young son to be in bed by 8pm but staying up later herself. Nor does the Elijah incident contradict such reasoning. The Lord could inspire his prophet to ridicule false belief as his spokesman without necessarily implying a general right to ridicule.

It's probably clear by now that I don't really know whether I have a 'right to ridicule' or not, because I'm not sure whether the concept really has a biblical basis or not. What I am sure of, though, is that Jesus Christ has given me the right to *be* ridiculed. This is a right of enormous worth, which he has granted to all his followers all over the world through all of time.

In this book, we will investigate what is meant by 'the right to be ridiculed', how we have such a right and why being on the receiving end of ridicule can actually be a positive experience.

CHAPTER ONE

No Surprise – Ridicule is to be Expected

While there are many passages of Scripture we could rightly explore in order to consider 'the right to be ridiculed', my intention is to focus on Matthew 5:11-12. These verses are so rich that we will approach them from many angles and yet still leave a great deal unsaid. You may well know the verses from memory, or perhaps you've looked them up in the past few moments, but let's look at them together in their entirety:

> *Blessed are you when people insult you, persecute you and falsely say all kinds of evil against you because of me. Rejoice and be glad, because great is your reward in heaven, for in the same way they persecuted the prophets who were before you.*

The first thing to be clear on is the fact that in these verses the Lord is expressing his will directly to all his followers. In other words, these verses bring the same message to believers in our context today as they brought to the initial readers of Matthew's Gospel, and indeed this is precisely the same message that was given to those who heard Jesus speak the day he gave this teaching. Not all verses of Scripture automatically express the Lord's will for all his followers in so direct a fashion. Matthew 10:10, for example, records the Lord Jesus instructing the twelve not to take a bag or extra clothing with them on the mission journey he was sending them on. Does this mean that people who go on mission journeys today shouldn't take any spare clothes with them? No. While this verse is certainly part of God's inspired word with much to teach us, it teaches us without obliging us to follow the precise instruction the twelve received for that particular trip.

How then do we know whether any given verse is binding on believers today? By letting it speak for itself, within the context of the passage and book it's found in. When this is done with Matthew 10:10, it becomes clear that the instruction it records was a specific one for the twelve on that particular mission trip. Believers today can rightly receive Matthew

13

10:10 as God's word and learn much from it without feeling obliged to literally observe its specific instructions. With Matthew 5:11-12, however, the context makes it clear that these verses are binding on all believers all the time. Matthew 5:1 shows that Jesus was addressing his disciples in general, and not just giving specific instructions to the twelve. Moreover, the commands given throughout the famous 'sermon on the mount' (which runs through Matthew 5-7) are stated in a way which makes their application to all believers obvious. No-one would seriously suggest that the Lord Christ no longer calls believers to seek first his Kingdom (6:33) or to treat others as they would like to be treated (7:12). Nor would anyone who accepts the authority of the word deny that Christians today are called to be salt and light (5:13-16) and to be peacemakers (5:10). Surely, then, there can be no doubt that the verses we're looking at now are directly applicable to all believers at all times in all places.

With that important preliminary out of the way, let's move on to consider the actual content of the verses. We do so with a particular focus on the idea of being ridiculed. Surely there can be no doubt whatsoever that the Lord Jesus here states that his disciples should be well aware that being ridiculed for their faith is a real possibility. Indeed, the verses give a striking indication that opposition which goes far beyond mere ridicule is to be expected by followers of Jesus.

The phrase 'because of me' at the end of verse 11 shows that the Master is talking about hardships that will come upon Christians *because they are Christians*. The verses are not about insults, persecutions and accusations that are levelled at people irrespective of their faith. Needless to say, Christians may well be among the victims of such general malice and are called to respond to it in a God-honouring way. These verses, however, are not just saying that believers are not immune from the mistreatment that people may suffer from the hands of others. Rather, verse 11 goes significantly further and asserts that believers will often face hardship simply because they are believers. It's striking, too, that the Lord used the word 'when' not 'if'. Could he have made it any clearer that Christians are to expect opposition?

Verse 11 by itself makes it clear that this interpretation is correct – the words simply demand to be understood in this way. If any doubt lingers, though, it can surely be removed by considering other parts of the New Testament. John 15:20 offers strikingly similar teaching, while giving a fascinating insight into what lies behind the teaching:

A servant is not greater than his master. If they persecuted me, they will persecute you...

Here the Lord once again warns his disciples to expect opposition, and he grounds this expectation in how the world treated him. If Christ himself suffered opposition, should his followers expect not to? Sticking to our specific topic, if Christ himself was ridiculed (as he most clearly was, especially during his suffering on the cross and the events that led up to it), should his disciples imagine that they will avoid ridicule?

Even a fleeting glance at the book of Acts and the epistles (not to mention Revelation) will show beyond all doubt that the earliest Christians did indeed experience opposition on a very frequent basis. Occasionally this seems to have been mere ridicule (as when some members of the Areopagus 'sneered' at Paul in Acts 17:32), though generally it was more serious. So common was this experience that Paul and Barnabas strengthened the converts of their first missionary journey by telling them, 'We must go through many hardships to enter the kingdom of God.'[1]

Key Lesson:

As believers, we should not be surprised if we are ridiculed for our faith.

Use

Each chapter in this book is concluded with a section entitled 'Use'. Puritan pastors used this word to mean more or less what we usually refer to as *application*. The reason I employ the term 'use' is that the Puritans majored on use much more than we typically do today, and in this I would suggest they were more in keeping with the New Testament than we are. In other words, I'm using what might seem like an older term to alert us to a fact previous generations of believers knew well and we may have forgotten – the fact that we haven't really understood any scriptural truth until we've seriously considered how it ought to change us.

Therefore, let us consider a number of 'uses' arising from this chapter.

---

[1] Acts 14:22

1. THERE'S NO NEED TO SPECULATE ABOUT THE LIKELIHOOD OF RIDICULE.

In some parts of the church in the Western world today there seems to be growing talk about the possibility of persecution. I've heard mature and sensible believers express the opinion that outright persecution will be a reality in the UK within a generation or two. With some this view is so strong that it should perhaps be described as a conviction, rather than merely an opinion. Other godly people seem to have a vastly different expectation of what the near future holds. Instead of persecution, they anticipate a great revival in our part of the world. Of course, these two views don't need to be mutually exclusive. Persecution and revival can go hand in hand to some degree, as the history of the church abundantly demonstrates.

Thinking in this kind of way about the future is not necessarily harmful. When done well, it can be a legitimate way of obeying the biblical command to be watchful[2]. There are some dangers inherent in it, though. One is that we might become so interested in speculating about what the future could hold that we neglect our calling in the present. It is possible to devote so much time and energy to contemplating days to come that we overlook what we're called to this day. If you have a detailed picture in your head as to what you're expecting the future to look like, yet you're neglecting to live in a gospel-shaped way in some element of life in the present, then you've fallen foul of this danger.

The truth of this chapter can help deliver us from this pitfall. We have seen, from Matthew 5:11-12, that as believers we should not be surprised if we are ridiculed for our faith (or indeed if we're opposed in the more serious ways that verse 11 details). The Lord has thus given us a clear warning that such opposition may come our way. Therefore, there is no need for us to speculate on the likelihood of such difficulties arising. Our role is to get on with walking with him and serving him now. By his grace we can do so, knowing that whether ridicule (or worse) comes or not, the Lord will give us the grace we need to keep on walking with him. Since the Lord has told us that opposition from the world may come, let's not get preoccupied with speculating about whether such opposition will come or not. Rather, let's get on with honouring him in the power of his Spirit!

---

[2] Colossians 4:2, for example

2. PRAISE THE LORD FOR HIS INTEGRITY!

Whenever you're trying to get somebody to do something, don't you tend to present that 'something' in the best possible light? For example, if you're trying to encourage your family members that it would be great to get a puppy, you'll probably talk to them more about fun and cuteness than you will about chewing furniture and toilet training. Sometimes this presenting of things in the best possible light is downright dishonesty, like when an estate agent chooses not to tell a client about a structural issue with a house they're viewing, or when a car salesman conveniently forgets to mention that the car the customer is interested in hasn't been serviced regularly. At other times it's not so blatantly dishonest, but it does tend to present a one-sided view of things – as in the puppy example. When you think about it, this kind of persuasion really comes naturally to us, and you're only likely to avoid employing it if you make a conscious effort to do so. Indeed, many would argue that there is no need to make such an effort, and that persuasion of this kind is fair and legitimate.

How different is the way of the Lord Christ! When calling people to be his followers, he did not use one-sided persuasion at all! He did not tell people about the benefits of following him but conveniently forget to mention the aspects of discipleship that were less likely to be appealing. On the contrary, he was astonishingly open about the cost of following him and the potential difficulties involved. This is one of the shocking yet glorious attributes of Christ which is so vividly revealed in the four Gospels. These verses are an example of it. Granted, in these verses he was talking primarily to those who already were his disciples. Nevertheless, his perfectly candid statement that they should not be surprised if they are ridiculed (or worse) for following him is indicative of the absolute integrity he displayed in calling people to be his disciples. Of course, he continues to call people to be his disciples today. He does so through his word and by his Spirit, and texts such as this show that he continues to issue his call with wonderful integrity.

Our next use will consider how this integrity ought to be reflected in our calling people to follow Jesus today, but before we go on to that, let's allow this truth to inspire us to praise the Lord! See the breathtaking honesty and integrity of the Lord Jesus Christ, and so give him glory!

17

3. PRESENT THE GOSPEL HONESTLY.

Praising the Lord for the unwavering integrity with which he presents the gospel should surely lead on to seeking to emulate that integrity ourselves, by his enabling grace. This is a use which has particular relevance to all who are regularly engaged in communicating the gospel to others, especially those who hold some sort of teaching position: preachers, youth leaders, Bible Study leaders and so on. While it might have particular application to those of us who hold such positions, it has something to say to everyone who seeks to share the gospel with others, however formally or informally they may do so.

Most of us who share the gospel regularly are surely eager to see people come to know Jesus as their Saviour. That is certainly right and good. No doubt, indeed, we could all rightly ask the Lord to give us a greater desire to see others put their trust in Jesus. Sometimes, though, our desire to see others respond positively to the gospel doesn't always spring from the best motive. Sometimes our motivation can be surprisingly selfish. Maybe we can't cope with the thought that a loved one doesn't profess faith, or perhaps we fear that our teaching ministry will be deemed a failure if it doesn't lead to a flood of conversions, so we become desperate for an outward response. Such an eagerness for a response – especially if our motives are not all that they might be – can lead to us trying to make the gospel 'more appealing'. Such a mistake would probably lead to us neglecting to tell people about the cost of discipleship and the potential for ridicule (or something worse) to come our way for following Jesus.

Let these verses, and the particular truth that we've drawn from them in this chapter, keep us from such a watering down of the gospel call. Christ himself was perfectly clear and open in presenting the potential cost of discipleship, and all who endeavour to make disciples in his name should do likewise. The Lord Christ no doubt knew that those to whom his gospel came with power, with the Holy Spirit and with deep conviction[3] would see that he is worth being ridiculed for and would respond positively despite the potential cost. May we who pass on the gospel today do so with similar integrity and confidence!

---

[3] 1 Thessalonians 1:5

4. SEE CLEARLY THAT HE IS WORTH IT.

In this chapter we have recognised that as Christians we should not be surprised if we are ridiculed for our faith; this message is very clear in the verses we have looked at. Why is the Lord so blunt and direct in warning his followers about the possibility of ridicule (or worse)? One reason, as we've noted already, is his faultless integrity – he knows the possibility to be real, and therefore he simply shares it openly and honestly. Another reason is that he wants his followers (and indeed those who are considering becoming his followers) to realise that though they may suffer for following him, *he is worth it.* However much ridicule (or worse) a believer may be exposed to, it is still vastly better to be with Jesus than without him. It is much better to suffer in his way than to have Christless comfort and ease.

Why is he worth it? This is the question that the rest of this book is devoted to. For now, let me encourage you to get it clear in your head and heart that *he is indeed worth it.* For various reasons this might be a timely message for you. Maybe you've just become a Christian and you're hesitant about telling your friends and family in case they think you're an idiot. Perhaps you're heading to university or college and you're considering keeping your faith secret in case your peers laugh at you. Maybe you're shying away from telling your work colleagues, your neighbours or your friends at the golf club about your faith for a similar reason. Many of us might be inclined to keep our faith private in case we get a hostile reaction from others. For most of us in the Western world, if a hostile response does come, it isn't likely to be anything more than ridicule. Hear the Lord's message! Should such ridicule – or even much more serious opposition – come our way, *he is worth it!* Ridicule may well come, but he is worth being ridiculed for!

CHAPTER TWO

Tough-going – Ridicule Hurts

One of the great dangers in talking about any kind of hardship is that of being too trivial and superficial. It's easy to talk about suffering in a glib sort of way that comes far short of doing justice to the depth of pain which people in the midst of that suffering are experiencing. This danger is perhaps particularly acute when trying to offer hope and comfort to those who are suffering – in an understandable eagerness to say something positive, we can unwittingly gloss over the reality of the difficulty.

While it's probably naive and foolish to compare forms of suffering to one another with a view to deciding which is the worst, just about everybody will surely agree that ridicule is not the most serious hardship a person may face. Nevertheless, it is sufficiently serious that we must take care to avoid talking about it in the sort of superficial way mentioned above. Before we go on to explore how being ridiculed for Christ is worth it, let's take time to appreciate that when he made these great statements about suffering for him, the Lord Jesus was not failing to take the reality of human suffering seriously.

Of course, the very nature of who Jesus is shows that he couldn't possibly be guilty of failing to take human suffering sufficiently seriously. To unpack this a little further, though, let's explore a little-known story that is recorded in 2 Chronicles 30. Three whole chapters in 2 Chronicles are devoted to how King Hezekiah endeavoured to restore the true worship of the LORD in the land, after the idolatrous reign of his father Ahaz (chapter 28). As part of these attempts at reform, he sent couriers throughout Israel and Judah urging the people to return to the LORD (verses 6-9). Verses 11 and 12 reveal that many responded positively to this message, especially in Judah. Verse 10, however, tells us that this good response was by no means uniform. Rather, the messengers found that in three tribal areas 'people scorned and ridiculed them'.

How do you suppose this made the couriers feel? In truth the text doesn't tell us precisely what impact the ridicule had on them, nor are we even told to what extent their hearts were in the task Hezekiah had set them. These are details which God has seen fit to leave unrecorded in his word, and we would thus be wise not to speculate about them. Without needing to engage in such speculation, however, surely the attentive and kind-hearted reader of the passage will find herself sympathising with the couriers. Imagine having so great and valuable a task entrusted to you and then meeting with such a withering response from some of those you were sent to! Even without knowledge of details beyond what the text records, surely we find ourselves feeling sorry for those ridiculed couriers.

No doubt the text is intentionally written in such a way as encourages this sympathetic response. Compassionate sympathy is the response that 2 Chronicles 30:10 will produce in the heart of the reader whose heart is truly engaged. Having established this, we can move on to ask some questions that link this passage to the verses[4] we are primarily studying. Do you think Jesus had read 2 Chronicles 30? Do you think he had understood it correctly? Do you think he would have understood it better than we do? Would he have felt sympathy for those who were ridiculed? Had he forgotten about this incident by the time he preached the Sermon on the Mount?

No doubt the answers to all these questions are strikingly obvious. The Lord would indeed have been familiar with the plight of the couriers in Hezekiah's day; no doubt he understood the text better than any other human being ever has, and the ridicule they faced would have met with a more compassionate and sympathetic reaction from his perfect heart than it ever has or ever will receive from any other human reader. Likewise, it's beyond all doubt that when he spoke about ridicule in Matthew 5:11-12, his compassionate sympathy had not been diminished and was not put on hold.

In other words, when Jesus Christ spoke about ridicule (or indeed any suffering for that matter) he was by no means guilty of any lack of realism. Such is the danger of being misunderstood that we needed to take this time to guard against even the faintest suggestion that there is any superficiality in what Matthew 5:11-12 says about ridicule. Even at this early stage of his ministry, prior to so much of his own suffering, Jesus' matchless heart of compassion and his perfect grasp of the Old

---

[4] Matthew 5:11-12

Testament were such that he could speak with true empathy about ridicule – more so, indeed, then anyone else possibly could.

So when Jesus told his disciples that it would be a blessing to be ridiculed for him, he was not suggesting that ridicule involves no real pain and is easily dealt with. On the contrary, he knew perfectly well that ridicule is not pleasant.

Key Lesson:

Ridicule hurts.

Use

1. DON'T UNDERESTIMATE THE CHALLENGE.

The primary aim in this book is to highlight that Jesus is worth being ridiculed for. A true sight of Christ will surely convince the believing soul that he is worth enduring the ridicule of the whole world for, and indeed much worse opposition besides. All the same, the challenge that lies before us is not to be taken lightly. That challenge is to have a love for Jesus and trust in him which won't shrink back in the face of ridicule; that will stand firm and even flourish in the midst of mocking. By his grace, such a close walk with him is certainly possible, and it's possible for 'rank and file' believers, not just for heroes of the faith. Hopefully the rest of this book will help us into such closeness with Christ (or indeed strengthen and deepen us in that closeness, if we already have it). For now, let's be clear that the challenge of being ridiculed is real, because ridicule hurts.

In other words, please don't misunderstand the message of this book. I'm not suggesting that if and when you're ridiculed for following Jesus, the insults will simply wash over you without causing you any pain, like water off a duck's back. That may happen in some cases, but for most (maybe even all) the ridicule will truly hurt. This may be especially so when the ridicule comes from family and friends. It may well reduce you to tears and leave you feeling isolated, upset and alone. In calling us to follow him despite the possibility of such ridicule, and in unashamedly asserting that following him will certainly be worth it, the Lord of glory was not denying that ridicule hurts. Let's not underestimate the challenge.

2. CARE FOR THOSE WHO FEAR RIDICULE.

Appreciating the challenge we face should naturally lead on to appreciating the challenge other believers face. Appreciating the challenge they face should in turn lead to us caring for them, and expressing that care in some appropriate manner. Above, we noted that we should be realistic about the fact that ridicule may hurt us; now we move on to consider what our attitude should be towards brothers and sisters who fear ridicule.

It's quite possible that some of the believers whom you know or come into contact with may fear ridicule significantly more than you do. This could be the case for all sorts of reasons, and it doesn't necessarily mean that they are less spiritually mature than you. It might be that they lack a close fellowship around them who would help them through ridicule. It may be that they've never really been ridiculed for anything before, and the unknown element makes the whole matter seem more terrifying. Or it might be that the thought of being ridiculed brings to mind a flood of bad memories. For all sorts of reasons, you may discover that some of your sisters and brothers find the possibility of ridicule much more frightening than you do. The fact that ridicule really does hurt shows that their fears are not to be dismissed lightly, so let's treat them with compassion.

This use may be particularly apt for those of us who are trying to help Christian children and young people in their walk with Jesus. We may be doing so as parents or other family members, as youth leaders, or in some other way. It's very possible that some, if not all, of these young people will fear the prospect of ridicule. In particular, they may be concerned that their peers will laugh at them for following Jesus. This could have a major bearing on their spiritual health and might lead to them 'hiding' their faith at school, university, work etc. Of course, we want to see them overcome this fear by the Lord's enabling might. As we seek to help them, however, let's appreciate how great their fears may be. By recognising that ridicule really does hurt, let's avoid taking a patronising attitude to those who fear it.

3. CARE FOR THE PERSECUTED PARTS OF CHURCH.

Given that ridicule hurts, we should compassionately care for fellow Christians who fear the thought of it. If that's true, doesn't it stand to reason that we should care for our persecuted brothers and sisters? Many around the world are facing not only the mocking jibes of others for Jesus but, moreover, hardships inflicted on them for their faith that are much more sinister than ridicule. Some are ostracised from their community, and even from their family. In some cases, this exclusion is so complete and final that they are essentially viewed as dead. Often this goes hand in hand with a loss of livelihood and possessions (which may well have been rather basic in the first place, so that they face a real struggle to survive). Some are imprisoned, and some even face martyrdom. Don't we have reason to care for them?

There is usually a difference between those who fear ridicule and those being persecuted. It's a difference which we may allow to have far too much significance. The difference I'm thinking of is this: those who fear ridicule typically have a reasonably close connection to us, but with those under persecution the connection is less obvious. Those we thought about in the previous use are often part of our church family, our social group or even our biological family. We know them personally, and it's not that hard to empathise with their concerns. Of course we care about them, and rightly so! Those we are thinking about now typically live a long way away from us, probably in a place we've never visited, and quite possibly in a country we couldn't locate on the map and might not even have heard of. The connection between them and us is not obvious, and it's not so easy for us to empathise with people we've never met, and whose context is so markedly different from ours. While the connection may not be immediately obvious, it is absolutely real! We are one family in Christ! Calling them our brothers and sisters in Christ is not merely a turn of phrase but an expression of fact! Let the truth that ridicule hurts inspire us to care for our family members who face much more than ridicule for the master.

4. SEE THAT IT'S STILL WORTH IT!

Most of us are familiar with the phenomenon of discovering that something is harder than we thought it would be and thus wondering if it's worth it anymore. Maybe you start eagerly into a DIY project and then realise that a fair bit more effort is called for than you had anticipated. Perhaps the appeal of greater fitness diminishes somewhat when the pain of prolonged exercise hits home. Any number of examples from everyday life could be given. Might this chapter be having a similar effect on you? Maybe the incident we explored in 2 Chronicles 30 has given you a fresh sense of what it's like to be ridiculed. Perhaps you're now beginning to wonder if following Jesus really is worth this potential cost.

It is!

CHAPTER THREE

The Great Reward: Joy

Having established that ridicule for the faith should come as no surprise to us as Christians, and indeed having noted that ridicule really does hurt, we're now in a position to get to the core of our subject and see that Jesus gives his followers something worth being ridiculed for. As we did in the previous chapter, we'll begin by exploring a different portion of Scripture and then return to Matthew 5:11-12. This time we look at a little couplet of parables in Matthew 13:44-46.

These two parables are both about the value of the Kingdom of Heaven. The Kingdom is compared to treasure hidden in a field and to a pearl of great price. In each instance, the man who discovered these valuable items 'sold all he had' in order to acquire them. The essential message is that Jesus is of such great worth that it would make sense to give up everything in order to belong to him. Disciples are certainly called to give up everything for Jesus (Luke 14:33) in the sense of submitting everything to his Lordship. This won't always mean actually losing every single possession, but it certainly means a principled willingness to sacrifice anything and everything for him. The point of these parables is that such giving up of everything is the sensible thing to do, because the Kingdom is of greater worth than anything and everything else you might have. The men who bought the field and the pearl were neither coaxed nor deceived; they willingly gave up what they had for the sake of something greater. So likewise, the disciple is to willingly submit everything to Jesus, who is greater than all things.

What does this have to do with ridicule? While we don't want to speculate about details which the parables do not include, doesn't it strike you that the actions of these two men might have seemed ridiculous in the eyes of onlookers? Of course, we're not told that there were any onlookers, but if you witnessed somebody sell everything he had in order to buy one field, would you not be inclined to think he was being a bit silly? We don't know how much the man owned, and it's perfectly possible that his 'everything' might just have come to the average price of a field. He might not necessarily have been silly in terms of the amount he paid for the field, but if that amount was truly his everything, you can surely see why that might be considered silly. No doubt you can imagine some less caring onlookers laughing at him and ridiculing him. Without daring to add anything to the parables, we can safely surmise that the actions of the two men who sold all that they had might easily have invoked ridicule from some. This is very much in keeping with the point of the parable, because giving up everything for Jesus is exactly the sort of action which invites the world's ridicule.

How do you suppose the men in the parables would have reacted to ridicule? Again, we don't want to speculate, but let me suggest that it wouldn't have bothered them too much. It might well have hurt them and saddened them, but it wouldn't have persuaded them to change their minds. Why not? Because they knew the value of the object they were selling everything for. To any who ridiculed them, it may well have seemed that the first man was extraordinarily foolish to sell everything for the sake of a field. He knew otherwise! He knew the field contained something of such value as would make his sacrifices worthwhile! You can rightly imagine him thinking, 'So what if people laugh at me? I know the field has value beyond what they've seen!'

By saying these things, we are not adding to the parable. Rather we are exploring its message in the sort of way it invites us to. Now its connection to Matthew 5:11-12 should be becoming clear. The man who sold everything to buy the field may well have been ridiculed for doing so, but he could rightly have taken such ridicule as a mere reminder of the fact that he knew the field to contain value which those who ridiculed him had not yet seen. So it should be with the disciple of Jesus who is ridiculed for following him. They may well be saddened and hurt by the ridicule, but they can rightly take it as a reminder that they have something of value which those who ridicule them seem sadly blind to: a relationship with Jesus and a place in his Kingdom.

Of course, they should desire that others (including those who ridicule them) will come to see the value of belonging to Jesus and will surrender their lives to him too. The parable of the hidden treasure and the pearl of great price might sound like they're saying, 'Take care of your own spiritual health and don't worry about others' (since the man who found the treasure 'hid it again', presumably to stop others getting it instead of him), but such a misinterpretation is a blatant example of pushing the word image too far. The point is to show the all-surpassing value of the kingdom, not to encourage some kind of spiritual selfishness.

While the committed disciple will be lovingly concerned for those who ridicule her, their ridicule will certainly not dissuade her in her walk with Jesus. Rather, the ridicule will serve to remind her of the all surpassing value of what she is ridiculed for. Thus, when Jesus urges his ridiculed followers to 'rejoice and be glad', he is not calling us to some sort of escapism. He is neither being unrealistic himself nor encouraging us to be unrealistic. On the contrary, he is calling us to real rejoicing in the present as we meet ridicule head on and realise afresh that what we're being ridiculed for is something of such value that if those who ridiculed us could only see it for what it is, they would lay aside their ridicule and give up everything to join us as disciples of his!

Key Lesson:

We can really rejoice when ridiculed for Jesus because the ridicule reminds us of the worth of what we're being ridiculed for.

Use

1. JOY AND SUFFERING CAN CO-EXIST.

Most of us tend to assume that a suffering person can't be a joyful person. We think that, though they might be a person who is generally full of joy, the reality of suffering will at the very least suspend their rejoicing. Therefore, we tend to conclude that suffering is to be avoided at all costs. This assumption is very prevalent in Western society today, so much so that once you're aware of it, you'll notice it cropping up again and again in the course of daily life.

The assumption is not entirely wrong. Naturally, no-one wants to suffer if they can avoid it, and the great world of joy that will be inhabited by all who belong to Jesus will be a world without suffering.[5] Therefore we ought not to be too dismissive of this very understandable viewpoint. Nevertheless, as disciples of Jesus we should still seek to avoid making this assumption ourselves, or at least to change it significantly. While the eternal joy of the believer will be free from all suffering, in the here and

---

[5] Revelation 21:4

28

now it is possible to experience the joy of the Lord *even when suffering*. This is not some sadistic sort of taking pleasure in the pain itself. On the contrary, it is a rejoicing in the Lord and in his good work in us even in the midst of pain. Much more could be said about this, but for the moment let's recognise this one truth clearly: *joy and suffering can be experienced by the same person at the same time.* The fact that one who is ridiculed for Jesus can yet rejoice points to this great truth.

2. AN INDICATOR OF TRUE DISCIPLESHIP.

The distinction between true disciples and false disciples is not a comfortable one for us to consider. It is an enormously difficult distinction to make if we're trying to do so with reference to somebody else (i.e. if we're trying to determine whether another professing Christian is the real deal or not). Judging whether someone else really knows the Lord or not by their way of life is something that many of us are tempted to do, which is perhaps why such strong warnings about judging others are found in Scripture. Yet the Bible states clearly that not all who profess to know the Lord really do.[6] Quite apart from the whole question of judging others, if we want to accurately assess our own spiritual health, we obviously need to take these warnings seriously. Perhaps this reality of being ridiculed for the faith can help us. If we can face ridicule for the Master and rejoice in him even though the ridicule may hurt greatly, this will surely go some way to assuring us of our spiritual health. On the other hand, if we can't face the prospect of ridicule for him, or if we can't see how someone could rejoice in him even when ridiculed, that might indicate that we need to check where we stand with the Lord. I'm deliberately being tentative in my language here, because our reaction to ridicule for the Master is only one of many gauges of our spiritual health, and we need to avoid making hasty judgments about ourselves (let alone others). It's entirely possible that a true and healthy disciple may still react badly to ridicule, because we all stumble in many ways (James 3:2). On the flip side, even a good reaction to ridicule may not necessarily be a guarantee of good spiritual health. All the same, here we have one indicator that can help us gauge the reality of our discipleship.

---

[6] Matthew 7:21-23, for example

3. KNOW IF YOU'RE BEING RIDICULED FOR JESUS OR NOT.

Just because you're a Christian and you're being ridiculed, it doesn't necessarily follow that you are being ridiculed *for Jesus*. It might be the case that there is some other reason for the ridicule you're experiencing.

Let's consider an example that is arguably about something more than ridicule. A Christian man was very keen to tell others about Jesus. He expressed this passion to evangelise in the workplace, talking to colleagues about Jesus all the time. That sounds great. Sadly, though, he spent so long evangelising that he never did any work. His colleagues soon began to suspect that his passion for sharing the gospel was actually a mask for a deeper passion – namely, for picking up his pay without doing anything to earn it! Whether his colleagues were right to suspect laziness or not doesn't matter for our present purpose. Eventually, his boss had to tell him to stop talking so much during work. The man took this as a form of persecution. It wasn't. The boss wasn't in the least bit worried what the man was talking about; he just wanted to make sure that conversation did not interfere with the day's work. The man could just as easily have been told off for talking about sport.

In a similar way, it might be the case that we are ridiculed for something other than our faith. We're called to handle such ridicule in a Christian manner too, which includes rejoicing in the Lord in the midst of it. Likewise, the Lord is the One who can truly comfort us in the face of all ridicule, whether for our faith or not. However, it's only being ridiculed for Jesus that gives us the joy of seeing the worth of what we are ridiculed for. Let's be careful not to claim to be victims of ridicule for the Lord when in fact we're being ridiculed for something else.

4. THINK OF WHAT YOU'RE RIDICULED FOR.

Assuming it is our faith we are being ridiculed for, what practical steps can we take to go about rejoicing? Recalling these words of Jesus from Matthew 5:11-12 would certainly be a good first step, so if, by the Lord's grace, we can commit these verses to memory, that will surely prove very useful if and when ridicule comes (and even if it never comes). Having said that, merely knowing, recalling or even reciting the verses is not the entirety of what the Lord calls us to here. We're called to go a step further and appropriate their truth in the power of the Holy Spirit. In other words, with the Lord's help we are called, when ridiculed, to proactively think of the One we're ridiculed for and his all-surpassing value! If the man in the parable who sold everything to gain the field with treasure in it was ridiculed for doing so, surely turning his mind to what the field contained would have helped him to deal with the ridicule and even to rejoice! So likewise, if we are ridiculed for our faith, let's allow it to give us a fresh sense of what value there is in the One we're ridiculed for.

CHAPTER FOUR

The Great Reward: Character

Having discovered that disciples of Jesus really can rejoice when being ridiculed for him, the next logical step is to think a bit about what we are called to rejoice in. Verse 12 of Matthew 5 answers this question by saying, 'Rejoice and be glad, for great is your reward in heaven.' What precisely is this heavenly reward? And can some of it – even a little foretaste – be experienced in the here and now? We won't necessarily discover a comprehensive answer to these questions in this book, but we will consider three aspects of this reward. While the full experience of each of these is reserved for heaven, something of each can be tasted in this world. These three facets of the great reward occupy our next three chapters.

Firstly, we consider the reward of character. Even a cursory reading of the Bible will reveal that God is greatly concerned about the character of his people. Indeed, the verses which we're focusing on in this book are one example of this truth. They are part of the long block of teaching which fills Matthew 5-7 and is typically referred to as 'The Sermon on the Mount'. While a great deal can be said about this sermon, anyone who reads it in its entirety will surely come away feeling that it expresses what sort of people Jesus wants his followers to be – in other words, what sort of character he wants his disciples to have. The warning given in Matthew 5:11-12 is undoubtedly an expression of this concern for character. Surely one of the reasons the Lord Christ warns his disciples to expect opposition is that he wants us to have such character as, by his grace, reacts well when opposition comes.

What sort of character is it that Christ wants his people to have? In a word, 'Christlikeness' – he wants us to have character that reflects his own! You can discover this truth by comparing the teaching in the Sermon on the Mount to Jesus' own earthly life as recorded in the four Gospels. Such an exercise will reveal that he himself flawlessly followed the moral standards he proclaimed. For example, consider how he modelled the attitude to opposition which he calls us to in Matthew 5:11-12. In all the opposition the Gospels record him facing, and in particular in the lead up to, and even on, the cross, he clearly lived by this teaching himself. If you're still in any doubt, the witness of other portions of Scripture is equally clear. Take Romans 8:29, for example:

> *For those God foreknew he also predestined to be conformed to the image of his Son, that he might be the firstborn among many brothers and sisters.*

However you may be inclined to interpret what this verse says about foreknowledge and predestination, surely what it says about God's desire for his people to be like his Son is beyond all dispute!

Do you consider becoming like Jesus to be a good thing? I most certainly hope you do, because the biblical answer to this question is in no doubt! The One who came to give us life to the full (John 10:10) came to make us like himself. The One who demonstrated his own love for us in dying for us when we were yet sinners (Romans 5:8) is the One who calls us to be like him in character. Surely the plan for you of One who was willing to bear your sin on the cross in order to rescue you must be in your best interests. In other words, coming to have Christlike character really is a reward – it's a great blessing that comes our way because of the gospel. The fullness of this blessing is indeed in heaven, but the first-fruits of it can be enjoyed here and now! Simply put, *becoming like Jesus in character is a great and gracious blessing!*

What does all this have to do with ridicule? One of the reasons why God allows his people to face ridicule for him must surely be that he intends to use our experience of such ridicule to help us become more like Jesus. His intention is that as we seek to honour him by the power of his Spirit in the face of ridicule, his inner work of renewing us in his likeness will go on apace. There is a wider New Testament basis for believing that the facing of hardship often has a role to play in our growth into Christlikeness. For example, the book of Hebrew makes the staggering statement that Jesus 'learned obedience from what he suffered' (5:8). This is not at all meant to imply that his obedience was somehow lacking before he suffered. Rather, it's meant to help believers (both the original readers and others since) to see that if our commitment to God leads to suffering, and if we learn to put God first through hardship, then we can take heart from the perfectly obedient one whose path through this world was marked with suffering. Plenty of other examples could be given of biblical teaching on how suffering can have a place in the fulfilment of our calling, and in particular our calling to become Christlike in character.

Thus, it's clear that one reason why the disciple can rejoice when ridiculed is that the Lord will use even that ridicule as part of his glorious work of remaking us in his image. The beautiful character of Jesus so vividly revealed in Scripture is something we get to share in! In heaven we will be like him forever, and the process of becoming like him goes on in the here and now! Even the hardships we face will be used by him to bring us further into his wonderful likeness! Often, he uses challenging circumstances to grow the fruit of the Spirit in our lives. Facing people who are hard to love (because they laugh in work or school when they hear us say we follow Jesus, or for any other reason) is often part of how Christ grows the fruit of love in our lives.

Key Lesson:

We can rejoice when ridiculed for Christ
because he uses that ridicule to shape us into his likeness.

Use

1. SEE HOW IMPORTANT CHARACTER IS.

This chapter has emphasised just how important character is in the sight of God. He is passionately concerned that his people come to be like Christ. This is not merely an incidental matter of little significance. It is in many ways central to the whole gospel! The whole purpose of the plan of redemption is that God may be glorified in having a people who are like his Son in character. Surely verses such as Romans 8:29 make this very clear. Yet is it something we have grasped clearly? As Christians, do we see how important our growth in Christlike character is to God? If someone asked us why Jesus came into the world, would we say to save sinners from their sin and make them like him? Or would character transformation be left out of our answer altogether? The truth that God might allow us to be ridiculed (or worse) in order to help us become more like Jesus should help us to see the importance of character more clearly.

'He does not willingly bring affliction or grief to anyone.'[7] He takes no pleasure in seeing us face ridicule. Indeed, you might rightly say that our being ridiculed hurts him more than it hurts us. Yet he is prepared to let us face ridicule in order that it might be used to aid our growth into Christlikeness. Surely that should fix this truth firmly in our hearts and minds: *our character is of great importance to God!*

2. WE'RE TO SEEK CHRISTLIKENESS.

Once we see how much importance God attaches to our character transformation, it makes sense to attach a lot of importance to it ourselves. It goes without saying that living as a disciple of Jesus and experiencing the fullness of life that he came to bring includes aligning our priorities with his. What he deems important, we should deem important. If he deems our becoming Christlike to be so important that it's worth letting us face ridicule (or worse) for it, then we should view becoming like Jesus as immensely important too. This calls for us to gladly and freely make Christlikeness our goal. It is to be the prize we press on to take hold of.[8]

This has relevance to the entirety of life. We're called to pursue Christlikeness at home, at work, in church and everywhere. We're called to set our sights on becoming like Jesus during all seasons, good and bad. What does this mean in terms of being ridiculed for Jesus? What should our objective and goal be in such circumstances? *To become more like Jesus.* There may be other facets to our goal, and more detailed consideration of how to respond to ridicule will come later in this book, but for now let's get to grips with the fact that becoming like Jesus is to be our goal.

3. SEE WHAT HEAVEN WILL BE LIKE.

One use among several at the end of one chapter in one short book is never going to adequately speak of what heaven is like, but the truth we've been considering in this chapter should inform and shape our understanding of it. What will heaven be like? Part of the answer to this question is that in heaven believers will be fully like Jesus in character, and so will live in love for God and love for one another. In other words,

---

[7] Lamentations 3:33
[8] See Philippians 3:10-14

realising how central Christlikeness is to God's plan for us can help us understand what heaven will be like and thus help us to set our hearts and minds on it.[9] In a wonderfully complementary way, understanding why Christlikeness matters can help us look forward to heaven, and looking forward to heaven can help us strive for greater Christlikeness. It's a bit like a sports player who is preparing for a long-awaited tournament – the more they practise for it, the more they look forward to it; and the more they look forward to it, the more they are willing to practise for it. It's the positive equivalent of a 'catch 22' or 'vicious circle'. What has this to do with ridicule? Well, if you're facing up to the possibility of being ridiculed for Jesus and wondering how you might cope with that (let alone become more Christlike as a result of it), allow this to help you. Look forward to the day when you will be fully like Jesus in character, realise that if ridicule for him does come he will use it to help prepare you for that great day, and let that help you pursue Christlikeness!

4. RELY ON THE HOLY SPIRIT.

Now might be the time for a use that could rightly be included in every chapter, and that is surely wrapped up with every call that the Lord gives to his people – namely, that we are to rely on the enabling strength of the Holy Spirit as we seek to live by this teaching. This book is not the right place to fully consider the role of the Spirit in Christian living, but surely it's beyond all doubt that believers are to consciously rely on Him as we seek to honour the Lord in the whole of life. Why else would we be told to 'be filled with the Spirit'[10], to 'live by the Spirit'[11] and to 'keep in step with the Spirit'[12]? Indeed, all these commands come from passages that are very much concerned with everyday discipleship.

The particular truth we've been considering in this chapter is one that surely shows us how much we need to rely on Him. If left to my own strength, will I remember how important character is to God? By my own ability, will I successfully set my sights on becoming more like Jesus? Through my own resources, will I allow the thought of being with Jesus in heaven to inspire me to pursue Christlikeness when I am ridiculed?

---

[9] See Colossians 3:1-2
[10] Ephesians 5:18
[11] Galatians 5:16
[12] Galatians 5:25

No, no and no! I will not manage these things on my own, and nor will you! These are things with which we most definitely need the Lord's enabling grace, which is given by his Spirit. As we seek to rise to the challenges this chapter has brought, lets consciously rely on God the Holy Spirit.

CHAPTER FIVE

The Great Reward: God's Family

Relationships with our fellow Christians are hugely important in God's sight. Of course, our relationships with other people are vital too. We're called to love our neighbour as ourselves (Leviticus 19:18) irrespective of whether they share our faith or not. Yet our relationships with our brothers and sisters in the Lord have an especially important place, as any number of Scripture passages show.[13] Indeed, heaven can rightly be thought of as the place where all who are present through Christ will live in complete love for God and love for one another. To put it another way, heaven is the place where all present will truly live by the great commandment (Mark 12:29-31). Hence Jonathan Edwards rightly described heaven as 'a world of love'[14]. Letting this thought inspire us to live in love for God and others (especially our fellow believers) now is surely part of what Scripture calls us to when it urges us to set our hearts and minds on things above (Colossians 3:1-2).

In the verses we're exploring from Matthew 5, the Lord Jesus seems to make some reference to this great truth of God's family who love him and who love each other. Part of his explanation as to why those who follow him can rejoice even when they face opposition is as follows: '...in the same way they persecuted the prophets who were before you.' In part, no doubt, the point of this statement is to undergird the truth that those who suffer for the Lord have a great reward in heaven. The full verse (12) reads:

> *Rejoice and be glad, because great is your reward in heaven, for in the same way they persecuted the prophets who were before you.*

---

[13] Galatians 6:10, for example

[14] 'A world of love' is a title in the *Pocket Puritan* series by Banner of Truth. It is an excerpt from Edwards' longer work entitled 'Charity and its fruits'.

The point of the reference to the prophets helps us appreciate the first half of the verse. Surely the Lord's meaning is this: 'If you find it hard to rejoice and to focus on the great eternal reward, think about the prophets who have already left this world. Many of them faced great opposition. Do you suppose they now regret standing for the Lord? Of course not! They are enjoying their eternal reward! Let their example help you rejoice when you suffer for me.' My paraphrase is poor compared to the Lord's own word, but I trust it helps us see the point: the example of the prophets should help believers rejoice in the face of opposition.

Thus, the main purpose of the reference to the prophets can be clearly seen, but it might have a little more to teach us still. The little phrase 'before you' is of great significance. One element of its meaning is a mere matter of time; the prophets spoken of had already run their race and fought their fight long before Jesus was speaking. In saying 'before you', however, the Lord was not merely urging his disciples to learn from godly figures of the past. He *was* doing that, but he was doing something more too. He was drawing a link between the prophets of old and his followers, and emphasising what they shared in common. As a minister, I sometimes tell people who ask me how my ministry is going that I'm enjoying the fruit of those who went before me i.e. the pastors who ministered here before I did. In saying that, I'm not just acknowledging the historical fact that they ministered in these congregations at an earlier date. Like Jesus, I am reflecting that they and I have more in common than merely doing a similar type of work in the same setting. So it is in this case of Matthew 5. In speaking of the prophets who came before his disciples, Jesus was speaking of a unity between his disciples and those prophets.

So what sort of unity is there between Old Testament prophets and disciples of Jesus? Much could be said about each sharing a similar task and facing the same sort of opposition. That's why the example of the prophets could help disciples of Jesus rejoice when mistreated for him. The unity between the prophets and the disciples, however, is more than just that of a common task or even a common threat. It is the unity we spoke of at the beginning of this chapter: the unity of belonging to the one true God and so belonging to one another as part of his family.

The unity at that time could not be expressed in terms of the two relating to each other, because the prophets were in heaven and the disciples on earth. Believers who have left this world and believers who are still in it cannot interact with each other in the way that they will do in the new creation, or even in the way that believers who are still here interact with one another. Nevertheless, they are all members of the one family. Some of the Scriptures we alluded to at the beginning of this chapter indicate this truth, and there are many more that do so too. For example, this truth is revealed in Paul's statement that all who believe are children of Abraham (Galatians 3:9). The Lord did not talk directly about all of this in Matthew 5:11-12; nevertheless, when we hear him speak to his disciples of 'the prophets who were before you', we can rightly conclude that he was (and is) reminding his disciples that they are part of God's big family.

This is very significant with regard to ridicule. One of the reasons why ridicule hurts is that it effectively serves to exclude us. If someone mocks us for our faith and most, if not all, of those present condone the ridicule with their laughter, often what causes much of the pain is the feeling that we're being rejected and we don't belong. None of us like being rejected, and we all desire to belong, so this is a real problem. How can we rejoice in the face of ridicule even when it heralds our rejection by others? In part because, according to this verse, that ridicule should remind us that we *do* belong – that we belong to a group whom it is most worthwhile to belong to, namely the family of God!

Key Lesson:

*We can rejoice when ridiculed for Jesus
because that ridicule reminds us that we belong to his family.*

Use

1. SEE HOW IMPORTANT FELLOWSHIP IS.

Without doubt God cares about us all as individuals. You are unique, he cares about you, and he calls you to a personal relationship with him through Jesus. That relationship is in many ways an individual and personal matter – you listen to him as he speaks in his word, and you speak to him in prayer knowing he lovingly listens to you. While other Christians can certainly help you with such things, and in your Christian living more generally, they can't do it for you. If your Christian life is to flourish, that is ultimately between you and God. In other words, God is certainly interested in you as an individual and not just as one tiny component of a much bigger whole.

However, God's love for you as an individual does not mean that your Christian life is to be lived in isolation. Quite the opposite! Yes, he cares about you as an individual. He has not, however, formed you and redeemed you for you to be entirely alone from other people. Rather, part of his glorious purpose for you is that you may have meaningful and mutually enriching relationships with others. This is an indispensable element of your spiritual health. There are many portions of scripture that show this, including the one we're exploring now. If belonging to God's family is significant enough to give us reason to rejoice in the face of ridicule, then fellowship with other believers is obviously of great importance. Let's allow this truth to convince us that fellowship matters.

2. BE WILLING TO LEARN FROM OTHERS.

Once we see how significant fellowship is, a whole raft of practical implications can quickly be identified. One is that we're called to learn from our brothers and sisters in Christ. Do take some time to think how other Christians might help you with the challenge of ridicule. If you're facing up to the prospect of ridicule, might there be other believers known to you who have experienced something similar? Could there be someone in your church who could tell you how the Lord brought them through ridicule, or hostility of some kind?

Thinking about this might lead you to realise that there are many Christians whom you *know of* (perhaps indeed you worship with them Sunday by Sunday) but whom you don't *know* very well. Here is an encouragement to go and take a genuine interest in them! Make a bit of an effort to get to know them. Chat to somebody you don't normally speak to at the cup of tea after the service. Do so, not just in the hope of hearing something from them that will help you, but with a sincere love for your sister or brother in the Lord. If you've ears to hear, you may well learn much from getting to know fellow Christians, and in God's good providence one or more of them might just give you the help you need to face ridicule.

Before we leave this use, allow me to again point to the persecuted parts of the church. Its members are just as much our brothers and sisters as the Christians in our own church family. Thanks to organisations like Open Doors, we can hear something of how the Lord helps his people through persecution. Listening to and learning from them could surely help us in many ways, including facing ridicule.

3. BE WILLING TO SHARE.

This use is perhaps the flip side of the previous use. Just as we can learn much from other believers as we get to know them, it's likewise possible for them to gain much by hearing of the Lord's work in our lives. This is an encouragement to us to be willing to share openly and honestly with our brothers and sisters and, in relation to the topic of the book, to share about ridicule or opposition we may have faced for our faith and how the Saviour enabled us to handle it. If we haven't faced any such opposition, maybe sharing a little of how the Lord has brought us through the ups and downs of life in general might help. While our story may not involve facing ridicule, any authentic sharing that relates the Lord's faithfulness and grace could be a great help to those who are facing ridicule for Jesus.

On this use of being willing to share, many of us will fall into one of two categories. Some of us are eager to share our own story, and some of us are reluctant to. We might not all fall into either of these categories, and some of us might alternate between the two, but our broad reaction to this use probably falls into one or other category for most of us. Those of us who are eager to share perhaps need to take care that our apparent desire to speak of the Lord's goodness to us isn't just an excuse to talk about ourselves and give others a good impression of us. I've made that mistake before and I'm probably not the only one. By all means, lets be eager to share about what the Lord has done for us, but let's make sure that our eagerness is genuine and that it's appropriately expressed. Those of us who are reluctant to share perhaps need a little encouragement. Telling others how the Lord has helped you does not need to be an arrogant thing (just like it doesn't require arrogance for one patient to recommend a doctor to another patient), and it may do more good than you could possibly hope. Let's be willing to share appropriately with our fellow believers!

4. DON'T RIDICULE EACH OTHER.

To some it might seem ludicrous even to mention this possibility, but this emphasis on fellowship helps us to see how terribly unfitting it would be for Christians to ridicule each other for their faith. I don't suppose anyone would deny the truth of this statement, but you might wonder why it needs to be made. Would Christians really ridicule their fellow Christians for their faith? Perhaps one believer would not earnestly and openly ridicule another for being a Christian (if they did so, this would surely prompt questions about their own profession of faith), but in a subtler way some believers can find themselves ridiculed by their fellow Christians.

For example, someone who is very zealous for evangelism can sometimes be laughed at for being a bit 'OTT', when really those laughing ought to ask themselves if their desire to see others come to Jesus is as strong as it ought to be. Something similar can happen with believers who are very earnest about prayer meetings, or about reading Scripture, or about social justice. It can happen with almost anything that they have a biblical basis for being earnest about. Sadly, we can attempt to justify our own apathy by making passionate disciples objects of ridicule.

In a similar way, believers can sometimes be ridiculed by fellow Christians who hold different views on secondary matters (infant baptism, for example). Often this 'ridicule' is meant to be light-hearted and humorous, but it can nevertheless end up having a discouraging effect. I'm certainly not saying that we can't joke about such things; cheerful banter between friends over their differing views can often do everyone good. We do need to be careful, though, that we don't inadvertently leave someone feeling ridiculed. If fellowship is to help us rejoice in the face of ridicule, how much should we ensure that we don't ridicule each other!

CHAPTER SIX

The Great Reward: The Speaker

A few years ago we were on a church youth group weekend by the beautiful shore of Lough Erne, County Fermanagh. One of our activities was a question and answer evening, in which the leaders did their best to answer questions from the young people on any and every subject. Since we had arrived at our accommodation, there had been a box available to place questions in so that they could be asked anonymously. All sorts of questions were asked; most (if not all) of the issues you would expect 21st century teenagers with church upbringings to be grappling with appeared in some form or other. All the serious questions (there were a few joke ones – no youth weekend would be complete without plenty of humour!) were good questions to ask, but one was particularly striking: 'What's the best thing about being a Christian?'

For us as leaders on that evening this question was a marvellous blessing! Amid the minefield of challenging and sensitive questions on tricky topics, here was an open invitation to the share the good news! In the years since, it has struck me that this question can likewise be a blessing when you simply ask it yourself and use it as an opportunity to reflect. All sorts of answers might possibly be given to it, and the answer which you would give in a year's time might not be the same as the one you'd give today. If I recall correctly, all the leaders answered it differently that night. Surely, though, there is one simple answer that surpasses all the others because it contains within it all the other good answers you might want to give. What is the best thing about being a Christian? *Knowing Christ!*

All the other good answers surely meet together in this one answer. You might say the best thing about being a Christian is knowing that your sins are forgiven, but you only know forgiveness because you know Jesus. Or you might say that the best thing about being a Christian is always having someone to turn to when you are most in need, but that too is only the case because you know the Lord. Or perhaps you'd say having a place in heaven is the best thing about being a Christian, but it will be spending eternity with Jesus that makes heaven heaven! Any number of other examples could be given. As surely as streams flow into the river, surely all the true answers to this question flow into this one answer: knowing Christ is the best thing about being a Christian!

Not only does this answer bring all the other good answers in along with it, it more importantly has a firm biblical basis. Any number of passages could be brought in to demonstrate this, but let's look at Philippians 3. In verse 8 the apostle Paul expressly says:

> *...I consider everything a loss because of the surpassing worth of knowing Christ Jesus my Lord, for whose sake I have lost all things.*

Here he shows us that knowing Jesus is so great that all the time he spent before knowing Jesus is to be viewed as 'a loss', despite all the credentials he listed in verses 5 and 6. Not only so, but he also makes it clear that if having a relationship with Jesus means losing everything else, Jesus is worth it. It's not surprising that he proceeds to say, 'I want to know Christ' (verse 10), even if the way to get to know him more is through 'participation in his sufferings'. Indeed, he proceeds to talk about how earnestly he was engaged in pressing on to know Christ more (verses 12-14). While the passage may not include the question, 'What is the best thing about being a Christian?' it surely gives us the apostle Paul's answer: *knowing Christ.*

Now let's bring all this back to Matthew 5:11-12, in which the Lord speaks of the great reward there is for those who suffer for him. We've discovered in previous chapters how this reward is partly experienced in the here and now, and how the supreme experience of it is reserved for heaven. We've likewise noted that change in character and a place in God's family are integral parts of it. Now we can talk about what the heart of the reward is: knowing Jesus. Jesus knows what is best for us and that real life for us truly consists in knowing him. That's why he said:

> '*...this is eternal life: that they know you, the only true God, and Jesus Christ, whom you have sent.*'
>
> *John 17:3*

In this verse the Saviour does not merely say that knowing God is what gives eternal life. Rather he says that knowing God *is* eternal life. It's only sensible to assume, therefore, that when he spoke of the great reward in verse 12 of Matthew 5, he was speaking first and foremost about a flourishing relationship with him. Only when knowing him is seen to be the very heart of the great reward are we truly doing justice to his teaching. Indeed, only then are we having a proper regard for who he is. To imagine that there could be a greater reward than knowing God is blasphemous nonsense.

If and when ridicule comes for belonging to Jesus, then we can rightly allow it to be a reminder that we do belong to him. He is worth being ridiculed for! If, in his goodness and grace, he uses the ridicule to draw us closer to himself, then that ridicule will have become an instrument of blessing to us.

Key Lesson:

We can rejoice when ridiculed for Jesus
because that ridicule reminds us that we belong to him.

Use

1. AIM TO KNOW JESUS MORE.

In Protestant circles we're generally quite good at stating clearly that Christianity is all about a personal relationship with Jesus Christ. In particular, when it comes to explaining the faith to non-Christians, we're usually quick to assert that it's a personal relationship with Jesus as Saviour and Lord that makes a person a Christian. Living by certain standards, being involved in church and so on are fitting and proper for Christians, and even in a certain sense 'necessary', but doing such things is not what makes you a Christian. Aren't we typically good at stating this to non-Christians? If indeed we are, I'm very glad that we are. My concern, though, is that we don't always hold on to this clarity when it comes to living our own Christian lives. We so easily fall into the trap of thinking that our Christianity lies in living a certain way or being involved in church activities and so on. We can very easily lose our focus on a personal relationship with Jesus and turn our Christian life into a mere list of programmes and activities, or a mere ethical code to strive towards. Without doubt our relationship with Jesus should express itself in our lifestyle choices and in our commitment to his church, but let's remember that a personal relationship with him is at the heart of authentic Christianity. In this chapter we've seen that knowing Jesus personally is so awesome that its worth being ridiculed for. Let that help us keep our focus on a relationship with him, so that our great desire is to grow in that relationship.

2. TALK TO HIM WHEN YOU'RE RIDICULED.

If you get ridiculed for Jesus later today, who will be the first person you talk to about it? If you've been ridiculed for him already, who did you turn to for support? For a great many of us, the answer to these questions probably isn't Jesus! Don't get me wrong, it is entirely right and proper to look to others to help us. Your first reaction might well be to seek the support of a good friend or family member. You may well turn to them for a shoulder to cry on. By no means whatsoever is there anything wrong with that. Looking to others, under God, to provide us with comfort is natural and fitting. Doubtless one of the major ways in which the Lord brings us comfort is through the means of other people. Surely, though, given that Christianity is all about a relationship with Christ, it makes sense to take time to talk to the Lord about the ridicule. Since knowing him is supremely what makes ridicule for him worthwhile, doesn't it make sense to unburden your heart to him about it? By all means let others help you. Speak to them about the ridicule directed at you so they may help. Don't forget to talk to the Lord about it though!

3. HELP OTHERS TO GROW.

Doesn't this chapter have much to say to those of us who attempt to offer support to someone who is ridiculed for Jesus? You might be called to do so as a friend, or as one outworking of your parental responsibilities, or in your role as a youth leader, pastor, elder or the like. When someone comes to you in distress because they've been ridiculed for following Jesus, what are you meant to do for them? What is your goal to be? Is it merely to comfort them, or might there be a little more to it? Comforting them is certainly something you're called to do, but is your aim just meant to be to cheer them up, or should you be endeavouring to do something more than that? What we've discovered in this chapter indicates that our aim should be to help them to grow in their relationship with Jesus. The goal is not merely to help them deal with the problem, but rather to help them to get closer still to the Lord. How you give care with this aim in mind will vary from situation to situation depending on all sorts of things – the circumstances of the person concerned, the nature of your relationship to them and so on. We won't look at these things in detail here, but should the Lord entrust us with the care of one of his ridiculed people, let's have this as our aim.

4. FREEDOM FROM FEAR.

Perhaps you've encountered people who seem to have no fear of ridicule. Maybe you've observed them endure a lot of mocking and it all seems to have no negative effect on them. There can be all sorts of reasons why people handle ridicule like this. Some non-Christians can doubtlessly handle ridicule very well. To be more specific, though, maybe you know some fellow *believers* who can handle ridicule really well. They can fearlessly engage in evangelism in potentially hostile environments. When ridicule comes, it seems only to strengthen their faith and enhance their witness. Perhaps you're not at all convinced that you would handle ridicule so well, and as a result you're fearful of the possibility. You would like to be free from this fear and to be like those fellow believers who aren't bothered by the prospect of ridicule. What can help you with this? One of the many possible answers relates to the message of this chapter: see that Jesus is worth being ridiculed for; see that he can use ridicule to help your relationship with him flourish. In light of these great truths, may his Spirit free you from the fear of ridicule!

CHAPTER SEVEN

Reacting in Worship

John Flavel may not be a name that you're familiar with. He was a puritan pastor in England in the 1600s. In a day and age of immense suffering, he endured hardships that were beyond the norm. Like many puritan pastors, he lost his income in 1662 when he was effectively forced out of the Church of England by the king. A few years later he lost both his parents in one go. They were arrested for attending a non-conformist prayer meeting and intentionally imprisoned in a jail where the 'great plague' was known to be rife. As their captors presumably intended, the plague took their lives. Perhaps worse still, Flavel's wife died in labour. The child died too. He remarried, only to be bereaved again. In fact, his third wife died too so that when he eventually died – in his mid-sixties – he was survived by his fourth wife. With that track record it's remarkable she was willing to marry him! Among Flavel's writings there is a relatively short book on bereavement, now published under the title *Facing Grief*. No doubt his personal experience helped to make him an author who could tackle so sensitive a subject in a helpful manner. What makes his book fascinating, though, is that his clear aim in it is not only to help grieving people cope, but also to help grieving people worship. His purpose in writing was not just to bring comfort (though he certainly sought to do that), but to inspire people to glorify God.

What has all of this got to do with ridicule? Just as our natural reaction when faced with bereavement may be to focus on ourselves and ask, 'How can I cope?', so when ridiculed our natural inclination might be to focus very much on ourselves. Likewise, just as Flavel sought to sensitively move his readers' focus from themselves to God, so the Lord Jesus in Matthew 5:11-12 sought to turn his disciples' focus from themselves to God. Those four words with which verse 12 begins – 'Rejoice and be glad...' – are a call to worship. They do not mean, 'Rejoice in being opposed.' That would be imbalanced. Nor do they merely mean, 'Keep your chin up.' That would sell the words short. They really mean *rejoice,* but rejoice in what? Or, more accurately, rejoice in whom? Rejoice in God! Rejoice in the Lord! Rejoice in the One whom you are facing ridicule (or worse) for! Just as Flavel aimed to show grieving people that they were first and foremost called to be worshippers, so here the Lord Jesus makes it clear that those who are opposed for him are called firstly to glorify and enjoy God.

Much can be said about how Christians are to respond when ridiculed for our faith. In some circumstances a significant part of our response might be to explain our faith clearly and show that it is not ridiculous, assuming that those who are ridiculing us are willing to engage in conversation. Whether such conversations are possible or not, there is no doubt that we are called to respond in love to those who ridicule us. Even they fall under the all-embracing commands to love our neighbour as ourselves and to do to others what we would like them to do to us. Indeed, Matthew 5 concludes with a very powerful call to love our enemies and pray for those who persecute us. Responding in a right way to those who ridicule us will be so much the more possible if we have loving fellowship with one another, so we could rightly talk about how to react together as a family of believers to ridicule (whether directed at all of us or just one member).

Some of these aspects of responding to ridicule will be spoken of in the coming chapters. Before anything can be said, though, about how we're to respond to others when ridiculed, we need first to see how we are to respond to God when we are ridiculed for him. Our response towards others is downstream of our response to him. While we might seem outwardly to make the right response towards others even if we haven't made the right response towards him, in truth a right response to him must come first. We can't really love our neighbours without first loving God, and that is as true when ridiculed as at any other time. It's this right response towards God which is to be at the heart of the disciple's response to ridicule, and it can be summed up in one word: worship.

In many ways what we are learning now is the practical conclusion that the previous chapters have been moving towards. Those who belong to God through saving faith in Christ Jesus have an abundance of reasons to rejoice in him. So many, indeed, that if we were to attempt to speak of all of them, there would be too many to declare. How many of these reasons are removed by the reality of ridicule? Not one! Being ridiculed for him does not make the wonder of his love any less great. Nor does it diminish the privilege of belonging to him. Nor does it impinge the blessing of having your sins forgiven. Nor does it detract from the beauty of his character. Nor does it remove the great sense of significance a true disciple can have. It removes none of these reasons to worship! If anything, in fact, it serves to bring them into sharper focus. The disciple who reacts well to ridicule will see even greater depth to these reasons for worship. No wonder, then, the Saviour urges his ridiculed people to 'rejoice and be glad'!

Key Lesson:

Ridiculed disciples are called to respond in worship.

Use

1. YOU'RE WELCOME TO WORSHIP EVEN IF YOU FEEL 'A MESS'.

There is a certain sense in which this chapter presents a very real challenge to us. Feeling excessively sorry for ourselves and indulging in a bit of self-pity can be very appealing and may very well form our initial reaction to ridicule. This chapter calls us to see that even when we are hurt, the world doesn't revolve around us, and that our purpose is to worship God even when we are ridiculed for him. This calling cuts directly against the grain of our remaining sinful nature, and therefore it is very challenging indeed. The challenge is so great, in fact, that we will never rise to meet it except by the mighty help of God the Holy Spirit. While the challenge is great, though, it goes hand in hand with a marvellous invitation. If you have just been ridiculed for your faith, you may well feel like an emotional mess, which is entirely understandable. You might be in tears. A whole range of emotions might be vying for control in your heart. Your head might be spinning, and you may feel unable to express yourself coherently. Will you need to get yourself sorted out before you can approach the throne of grace? Certainly not! Do you have to 'pull yourself together' before you can seek the king of kings? Emphatically no! He is more than willing to receive your worship just as you are. The call to worship when ridiculed is certainly challenging, but it's an awesome invitation too! If and when we are ridiculed for our faith, let's not decline it.

2. WHERE THE REAL BATTLE HAPPENS.

If and when ridicule for following Jesus comes your way, it may well feel like you've been involved in a battle. Hopefully, there won't have been any physical violence, but there may well have been plenty of aggression and you could certainly feel wounded. It's only natural that you'll want to see those wounds heal, and that is proper, good and right. However much the experience of being ridiculed may feel like a battle, though, there is a battle going on at a deeper level. It is the battle that takes place within the heart and that is going on in each true believer on a constant basis (though the intensity of it does seem to ebb and flow). The battle is all about this question: will you glorify and enjoy God or not? The two warring sides can legitimately be thought of as your remaining sinful nature (which of course the Devil seeks to take advantage of in every way possible) and the Holy Spirit (Galatians 5:17). This internal spiritual warfare has much to it, but we will focus on the fact that how you react to ridicule is more of a battleground than the outward circumstance of being ridiculed. The evil one doesn't aim to bring ridicule your way just because he likes to see Christians suffer (although that is presumably true). His aim is much deeper; he wants to stop you worshipping. In contrast, God wants not only to help you deal with ridicule but also to enable your joyous worship to be enflamed by it. We all know which of the two it's best to co-operate with!

3. CARING FOR RIDICULED BELIEVERS.

In the previous chapter we saw that when the Lord gives us the privilege of caring for our ridiculed brothers and sisters, we're to aim at helping them grow in their walk with him. What we've discovered in this chapter helps us understand that a bit more fully. How will the ridiculed believer grow? How does any believer grow? As they become more and more of a worshipper! That is, as they, by God's grace, seek more and more to glorify and enjoy him – in the directly spiritual matters such as prayer and Bible reading, and in the entirety of life. Helping a ridiculed believer grow really amounts to helping them worship (in the broad sense of the word). I'm certainly not suggesting that when a ridiculed brother or sister comes to you for comfort, you bluntly tell them just to 'worship and it'll all be grand'; this aim isn't to be pursued in so crude and uncaring a fashion. Nor am I attempting to give any practical direction on how you may go about this; that will vary a great deal depending on the person concerned, the nature of your relationship with them, etc. Rather, I am emphasising that that the goal of our care should be *to help them worship.* Let's certainly show care and compassion by the barrel-load, but let's aim to do something more than merely cheer them up; let's aim to enflame their worship!

4. HOW IMPORTANT TIME ALONE WITH GOD IS.

I'm sure you're familiar with the idea of a 'quiet time', even if you know it by another name. Spending time alone with God to listen to his word and speak to him in prayer – ideally on a daily basis – is generally seen as an indispensable part of Christian living, at least in evangelical circles. Of course, we can fall into all kinds of mistakes about this: we can do it legalistically (i.e. because we feel we 'have to'); or we can do it as a mere matter of routine (just 'going through the motions'); and so on. The fact that it can be done badly, though, is not a reason to conclude that it shouldn't be done at all. There are many excellent reasons to strive for quality time with God each day, and this chapter highlights one of them. We've seen that we are called to worship all the time, even when we are victims of something as unpleasant as ridicule. If and when ridicule comes, it most likely won't be easy to respond in worship. To do so we will certainly need the gracious help of the Holy Spirit there and then. All the same, if we are in the regular practice of spending time alone in worship, won't we be so much readier to face this challenge?

CHAPTER EIGHT

Reacting in Fellowship

The story goes that a minister was visiting a member of his congregation who hadn't attended church in a while. The man was fit and able to be at worship and professed to be a Christian, but for whatever reason had stopped attending. When the minister asked him why, he was initially defensive: 'It's all about a personal relationship with God. I can worship on my own at home.' It is true that being a Christian is about a personal relationship with God, and it's wonderfully true that worship on your own at home is not only possible but moreover very important; however, that does not mean that joining with others in worship can be neglected. The minister no doubt knew this and could have answered the man accordingly, but instead he took what might seem a more eccentric approach. It was winter time and the two men were sitting by the fire. The minister reached over and removed one of the hot coals with the tongs and set it down on the fireplace. The two men chatted on about other things, and before too long the coal that had been removed fizzled out, whereas the others were still red hot.

I've heard various versions of a story along these lines, and you may well have too. Whether it really happened or not, I can't say, but at any rate it illustrates a very powerful point. Just as one piece of coal will not continue to burn for very long when removed from the others, so one individual Christian who neglects fellowship with others runs the risk of dwindling spiritual health – they may no longer burn so brightly for Jesus.

It's possible to push this analogy too far. Some believers in some parts of the world have no access to fellowship, and of course God is able not only to sustain but indeed to enflame their spiritual life. That said, though, having no fellowship available to you is a very different thing from wilfully neglecting fellowship. On the flip side, merely doing things with other Christians or even attending church regularly will not automatically safeguard your spiritual health. If your church attendance is all outward act and no inward reality, it is more likely to hinder your spiritual health than help it. Nor should the analogy be pushed so far as to imply that a truly converted person will lose their salvation if they neglect fellowship. The whole question of falling away and eternal security is hugely important, and at the same time quite complicated. For my own part, I'm very happy to recommend chapters 17 and 18 of the Westminster Confession of Faith as helpful summaries of the Bible's teaching on this vital matter. The coal story can certainly be understood in a way that is in keeping with them. While it might need to be qualified in various ways, the coal analogy nevertheless points to something of undeniable truth: fellowship is crucially important to the Christian life. Hebrews 3:13 on its own would be enough to prove this point:

> *But encourage one another daily, as long as it is called 'Today',*
> *so that none of you may be hardened by sin's deceitfulness.*

If fellowship is of such importance, generally speaking, is it not all the more important when you are ridiculed for your faith? The verse we have just quoted speaks particularly about encouraging one another, and it at the very least suggests that we all need daily encouragement. How much more, then, are we likely to need encouragement when we are ridiculed? If we go back to the coal analogy, the ridiculed believer could be likened to a coal that is having some wind or water come its way. Having others around it will leave it much better placed to withstand this. Surely, then, seeking good fellowship is a very fitting element of our response to ridicule. Ultimately our primary concern is to respond in worship, but fellowship will often be a vital aid to doing so.

Does all this have anything to do with Matthew 5:11-12? Yes! For one thing, we can legitimately say that fellowship is to have an important place in helping us act upon the command given in these verses. Beyond that, the verses themselves seem to hint at the importance of fellowship: they are addressed to the disciples collectively and the words 'you' and 'your' are plural, and one facet of the great reward is belonging to God's family. Thus, we can very safely say that believers are to act on these commands together.

Realising this might help us get to grips with the practical outworking of the verses. For example, you might be ridiculed for your faith and feel a million miles away from rejoicing. Yet another Christian might witness the incident and be greatly encouraged by the godly way in which you handled it. This could cause them to rejoice, and if they then come and tell you what a good impact you had on them, that might very well help you to rejoice. All sorts of examples of this sort could be given. The powerful command of our Lord and Saviour in these verses can be more readily obeyed when we seek to help one another.

Key Lesson:

Ridiculed disciples are called to respond in fellowship.

Use

1. DON'T NEGLECT FELLOWSHIP.

Even when we are not experiencing ridicule or going through anything else unpleasant, there can be a temptation to neglect fellowship. We can easily be so individualistic that, irrespective of what our circumstances are like, we overlook the importance of fellowship. This general temptation, however, can often become a more particular issue when we face some kind of struggle, such as being ridiculed for our faith. Whenever you're facing a problem of some sort, and are perhaps feeling down about it, it can be easy to conclude that this justifies not going to church and interacting with other believers. Although there is no logical reason why it should justify neglecting fellowship, the tempter tends not to rely on logic. If he knows the ridicule has hurt you and has potential to have a negative impact on your walk with Jesus, he will seek to press home his advantage by keeping you away from what might help you, including fellowship with other believers. Thus, after experiencing ridicule for your faith, you might find yourself reluctant to go to church (perhaps especially so if going to church is the particular thing you were ridiculed for in the first place). If and when you're in this position, let the truth we have considered in this chapter expose the devil's trap and encourage you not to neglect fellowship.

2. ASK THE LORD FOR GOOD FELLOWSHIP.

You may perhaps have read this chapter thus far and thought, 'That makes sense, but we don't really have any fellowship in my church.' Maybe you're in a congregation were nobody really speaks to each other before or after the service. People just come in and go out in silence, and there's no real interaction with each other at all. You're certainly having fellowship in that you are worshipping together, but there's no obvious opportunity for you to get to know another believer in the sort of way that would make the kind of fellowship we've been talking about in this chapter possible. Or maybe there is some conversation before or after the service, but it only ever seems to be about football or shopping or the weather. Of course, it's perfectly fine to talk about such things, but the conversation never seems to move beyond superficial subjects, and there's no sign of someone offering you a word of encouragement or telling you that they'll be praying for you. Having read this chapter to this stage, you might well feel that you lack real fellowship. What should you do? Surely asking the Lord to give you good fellowship could rightly be an ongoing priority in your prayers. As part of your willingness to be part of the answer to your own prayers, you could proactively seek to offer fellowship to others by giving a word of encouragement when appropriate, for example. Pray for fellowship and practise fellowship!

3. LEARN FROM THE PERSECUTED.

It's probably not the case that you can have fellowship with persecuted brothers and sisters in quite the same way as you can with people in your own congregation. Even through a great organisation like Open Doors it might not be possible for you to have much contact with a persecuted believer. While your fellowship with them might only be indirect, it could nevertheless do much to help you when you are ridiculed for the faith (and even when you aren't). If, for example through a charity, you hear of disciples who have suffered incredible things for Jesus and have found their relationship with him deepened as a result, couldn't this do much to help you respond in a godly way to ridicule? If you were to read or hear of brothers and sisters who have practised the command, 'Rejoice and be glad,' even in the face of death, couldn't that stimulate you to follow the same command in the Spirit's power? By all means let's have good fellowship with Christians in our own sur-roundings, but let's not neglect fellowship with those persecuted for Jesus in other parts of the world – how much he may teach us through them!

4. SUPPORT THE PERSECUTED.

While we can and should learn from persecuted Christians – not least when we're facing ridicule – they are obviously not just a resource for our encouragement, they are our family members whom we should care for. There are various ways in which this can be expressed. Financial support can do much to provide for their material needs and make representation to government bodies on their behalf. You can also engage in a bit of advocacy yourself by contacting your political representatives and urging them to do all in their power to aid persecuted Christians. You can also sign petitions on their behalf and encourage others to consider doing so too. Your congregation or denomination may provide opportunities along these lines. Most significantly of all, you can pray for the Lord to strengthen and comfort them, to remove their persecutions and to bless their persecutors by bringing them to Jesus in repentance and faith. Again, your church or a para-church organisation might provide guidance and information so that you can pray for particular matters and particular people. I'm not legalistically suggesting that you need to do all these things on an ongoing basis, but if we benefit from the fellowship of persecuted brothers and sisters, shouldn't we be willing to show some fellowship to them?

CHAPTER NINE

Reacting in Love

Any reader of the New Testament will be in no doubt that the apostle Paul has a major place within it. He's identified as the author of 13 of the 27 New Testament books, and there's good reason to believe that he had significant influence in the writing of some of the others. In the book of Acts, which provides a history of the early church, he is in many ways the central character for more than half of the narrative. It is not quite right to deem him the central character, because the book of Acts is carefully written to show that Christ himself is the central character, even after his ascension to heaven. Under Christ, though, Paul had a pivotal role in the expansion and growth of the church – not only through his written teaching (usually to congregations or pastors), but also through his taking the gospel to places it had never reached before. If Acts is the record of how the good news began to bear fruit to the ends of the earth, then the apostle Paul was a prime instrument which the exalted Lord used to make this happen.

Paul was the most unlikely candidate for so major a role. Opposition to the spread of the gospel is an almost constant feature of the record in Acts (which no doubt has significant implications for all generations) and at one time Paul, known then as Saul, was the most ardent enemy of the church.

> *...Saul began to destroy the church. Going from house to house, he dragged off both men and women and put them in prison.*
>
> *Acts 8:3*

His dramatic change is perhaps one of the best-known incidents in the whole Bible. Even people with little interest in the Scriptures often know how he saw the light on the road to Damascus. He 'saw the light' in the fullest sense – he had a direct personal encounter with the Light of the World, Jesus Christ. His conversion is recorded in Acts 9, and twice later in the book (in chapters 22 and 26) he is recorded speaking about it in some detail. With all three of these accounts, we can build a fairly full picture of what happened that day.

Thankfully, we can also get some insight into what was going on in Paul's heart and mind prior to his encounter with Jesus. In Acts 26:14, we discover that the risen and exalted Lord said to Saul, 'Why do you persecute me?' and continued by saying, 'It is hard for you to kick against the goads?' This fascinating statement seems to suggest that Saul had already had some sort of encounter with the truth, and that he was stubbornly resisting it. Surely his 'kicking against the goads' was none other than coming face to face with the truth and power of the gospel and desperately rejecting it. If this interpretation is correct, we would expect to find that Saul's persecuting of the church was kick-started by coming face to face with a mighty Christian witness. That's precisely what we do find in Acts chapters 7 and 8! A mighty persecution of the church, with Saul as its ringleader, began on the same day that Stephen became the first Christian martyr (Acts 8:1-2). Stephen's witness was a remarkable one indeed. After an astonishing summary of the Old Testament that his adversaries were powerless to answer (Acts 7:2-53), Stephen was stoned to death (Acts 7:54-58). His Christlike attitude to his impending death complemented his verbal witness beautifully. He not only entrusted himself to the exalted Lord (verse 59), he also prayed for the forgiveness of those who killed him.

Saul was a willing contributor to this despicable act (Acts 7:58 and 8:1), and in his case Stephen's prayer was clearly answered in a most remarkable way! Surely there can be little doubt that the marvellous witness which God enabled Stephen to give led to Saul kicking against the goads and was part of God's preparing him both for his conversion and for the amazing ministry that followed it.

All of this is very striking in itself, and greatly helpful to our study of Matthew 5:11-12. Why? Because Stephen had clearly taken to heart the Lord's teaching in these verses (along with teaching recorded later in Matthew 5 about loving our enemies) and allowed it to shape his reaction to his harrowing circumstances. How could Stephen have reacted with such love and compassion to those who were killing him, unless he knew that, 'Blessed are you when people insult you, persecute you and falsely say all kinds of evil against you because of me...'? Whether he had access to these words in written form or simply by oral teaching from the apostles is an interesting academic question, but whatever the answer to it may be, our present conclusion stands: Stephen reacted in love to his persecutors because he knew the truth of Matthew 5:11-12.

The same truth is meant to inspire Christians today to react in love to those who oppose us. Within the limited scope of this book, we can safely say that when ridiculed for Jesus, we're called to respond in love to those who ridicule us. We're certainly called to respond in worship and fellowship, as the previous two chapters have shown. We're similarly called to respond compassionately to those who ridicule.

Key Lesson:

Ridiculed disciples are called to respond in love.

Use

1. WHAT A WITNESS THIS CAN BE.

I have been challenged by writing the doctrine section of this chapter, and surely you must have been challenged in reading it. Reacting in love to those who hurt us, even if the hurt is caused simply by words aimed at ridiculing us rather than by hurling stones at us to kill us, is obviously something no-one would find easy. Before we get too caught up in thinking about the challenge, however, let's take a moment to consider how great the witness could be. If you encounter someone who endures mistreatment and responds only with kindness, it's almost impossible not to respect their strength of character and their compassion. Say, for example, you wanted to have an argument with someone and for this reason said something provocative to them. If they responded in a gracious and loving way, wouldn't it be hard for you to stay mad at them? When someone is able to repay hatred with kindness, it is very natural to respect them. If they explain what it is that enables them to respond so remarkably, those who are listening are probably more likely to pay attention now that they've seen such admirable character. It doesn't mean, of course, that if we respond in love to those who ridicule us, all who witness it (including those who did the ridiculing) will automatically give their lives to Jesus. What it does mean, though, is that such a loving response to ridicule would be a mighty witness and, as such, could well be part of the Lord's way of bringing people to himself. Let's not underestimate the challenge, but let's not underestimate the potential witness either.

2. SEE RIDICULE AS AN OPPORTUNITY.

Much of the teaching in the Sermon on the Mount[15] can be said to turn your perspective upside down, although of course it would be more accurate to say that it turns it right-side up! In these chapters, Jesus repeatedly calls his followers to view various things in a way that is the opposite of the world's outlook. From what we have already discussed, we can see that ridicule is something the Lord wants us to have a radically different perspective on. Ridicule certainly isn't pleasant and obviously you'd prefer to avoid it, providing there was an appropriate way to do so. At the same time, however, it's not something to be unduly feared, nor is it something to be avoided at all costs. In fact, it can be a great opportunity to shine for Jesus and point others to him. This might be especially so if most of the non-Christians you know are lovely, decent people whose outward life is generally in keeping with biblical teaching. Among such people, the deep inward differences between you and them might not be immediately obvious in the typical course of day-to-day life. If ridicule arises and you respond in godly love, however, this might bring the inward differences to the surface and show your non-Christian friends and family members that they need Jesus. See ridicule as an opportunity!

3. RE-ALIGNING OUR PRIORITIES.

The above serves as one example of the fact that Jesus wants to change the priorities of his people so that they become more and more in line with his. In particular, he wants us to be people who increasingly value the glory of God and the good of others (especially their spiritual and eternal good) over our own immediate comfort. He wants us to be willing to face the unpleasantness of being ridiculed if it will advance the glory of God and be a blessing to others. He wants us to be people who realise that bringing glory to God and bringing blessing to others is a great blessing to us, irrespective of what we might need to endure in order to do so. He wants us (as we saw in a previous chapter) to be people who see growth in Christlike character to be a reward that exceeds the cost of

---

[15] Matthew 5-7

suffering for him. He wants us to have priorities that are radically different from the world because they are actually in sync with his. The call to react in love is a reminder of the wider call to realign our priorities with his.

4. RELY ON HIS SPIRIT ALWAYS.

The previous three uses have shown that while this doctrine is very challenging, it ought not to be perceived as something negative. It is only right to view it in the very positive light which it deserves. Yet the challenge should not be overlooked either. If you already have fellow students, colleagues or members of your sports team who laugh at you for following Jesus, you're likely well aware of how great the challenge can be. Or perhaps in reading this, you – like me – have no reason to believe that you're going to be ridiculed for Jesus anytime soon. But suppose you are. Suppose ridicule arises unexpectedly, maybe even from a person you know and trust. Suppose it's carefully calculated to be as hurtful as possible. Suppose a whole crowd of people join in and, humanly speaking, you're left on your own. Could you be confident that in your own strength you would react in love? Could I? Left to our own resources, would we react in a manner that resembled Stephen's attitude to his killers? I hope none of us say yes! I hope we don't imagine we can meet this challenge in some strength of our own. Surely we can't. Nor do we have to. Stephen was able to respond in such love because he was full of the Holy Spirit (Acts 6:5). For you and me to react in love in response to ridicule (and indeed to live truly for Jesus in the general course of life) we too need the help of God the Holy Spirit. Therefore, the challenge of this chapter calls us afresh to consciously rely on the Holy Spirit always.

Conclusion

I still haven't worked out whether I have a 'right to ridicule' or not. I suppose it all comes down to what you mean by ridicule. If what you term 'ridicule' flows from a compassionate desire to do the person good and is maybe even meant to be appropriately humorous for them, then perhaps such ridicule could be justified. On the other hand, if there's no desire to do good to those whom you're ridiculing then it's hard to see how there could ever be any legitimate right to do so – especially if you're aiming to gratify yourself or to make money at their expense. Even this distinction, however, seems to generate more questions than answers. How can we judge if ridicule is well intended or not? If ridicule isn't well intended, what, if anything, should be done to try to discourage it? If as a society we acknowledge a 'right to ridicule' then who gets to determine what is ridiculous? Who decides, and on what basis, what is or is not a legitimate object of ridicule?

All these are fascinating and important questions. Studying Matthew 5:11-12 may not have answered them, but it's achieved something much more important. It's shown us that Jesus Christ has given us the right to *be* ridiculed for him, because he is the Lord, and that walking with him – whatever the cost – is true and eternal life.

> *Blessed are you when people insult you, persecute you and falsely say all kinds of evil against you because of me. Rejoice and be glad, because great is your reward in heaven, for in the same way they persecuted the prophets who were before you.*

Summary of Key Lessons

1. As believers, we should not be surprised if we are ridiculed for our faith.

2. Ridicule hurts.

3. We can really rejoice when ridiculed for Jesus because the ridicule reminds us of the worth of what we're being ridiculed for.

4. We can rejoice when ridiculed for Christ because he uses that ridicule to shape us into his likeness.

5. We can rejoice when ridiculed for Jesus because that ridicule reminds us that we belong to his family.

6. We can rejoice when ridiculed for Jesus because that ridicule reminds us that we belong to him.

7. Ridiculed disciples are called to respond in worship.

8. Ridiculed disciples are called to respond in fellowship.

9. Ridiculed disciples are called to respond in love.